D0948934

I LOVE TO BRUSH MY TEETH

أُحِبُّ أنْ أفرُشَ أَسْنَانِي

Shelley Admont
Illustrated by Sonal Goyal, Sumit Sakhuja

www.kidkiddos.com

Copyright©2015 by S. A. Publishing ©2017 by KidKiddos Books Ltd.

support@kidkiddos.com

First edition, 2017

Translated from English by Amelie Meryssa

قامت بترجمة هذه القصّة من الانجليزيّة: أمل مريصة

Arabic editing by Tahani ALi and Fatima Bekkouche

Library and Archives Canada Cataloguing in Publication

I Love to Brush My Teeth (Arabic Bilingual Edition)/ Shelley Admont

ISBN: 978-1-5259-0470-7 paperback

ISBN: 978-1-5259-0471-4 hardcover

ISBN: 978-1-5259-0469-1 eBook

KidKiddos Books

For those I love the most

لأحبائي

Morning came and the sun was shining in the faraway forest. There, in a small house, lived little bunny Jimmy, with his parents and two older brothers.

حَلَّ الصّباحُ وأَشرَقَتِ الشَّمسُ في الْغابةِ الْبَعيدةِ، حَيْثُ كانَ يَعيشُ الْأَرنبُ الصَّغيرُ جيمي مَعَ والِدَيْهِ و أَخوَيْهِ الْأَكْبَرِ سنّاً في مَنْزِلٍ صَغير.

Mom came into the room that Jimmy shared with his brothers.

دَخَلَتِ الْأُمُّ إِلَى الْغُرْفةِ الَّتي يَتَقاسَمُهَا جيمي مَعَ إِخْوَتِه.

First she kissed the oldest brother, who slept peacefully in his blue bed. Next she gave a kiss to the middle brother. He was still sleeping in his green bed.

أَوَّلًا، قَبَّلَتِ الْأَخَ الْأَكْبَرَ الَّذي نامَ بِهُدوءٍ عَلَى سَريرِهِ الْأَزْرَقِ. ثُمَّ أَعْطَتِ الْأَخَ الْأَوْسَطَ قُبْلَةً بَيْنَمَا لا يَزالُ نائِمًا على سَريرِهِ الْأَخْضَر.

Finally, Mom went to Jimmy's orange bed, and gave him a kiss.

و أَخِيراً، تَوَجَّهَتِ الْأُمُّ نَحْوَ سَرِيرِ جِيمِي الْبُرْتُقَالِيِّ و أَعْطَتِ الْأَرْنَبَ الصَّغِيرَ قُبْلَةً.

"Good morning, children," said Mom.
"It's time to rise."

قَالَتِ الْأُمُّ: "صَبَاحُ الْخَيْرِ يَا أَطْفَال، إِنَّهُ وَقْتُ النُّهُوضِ."

Getting out of bed, the oldest brother made his way to the bathroom.

نَهَضَ الْأَخُ الْأَكْبَرُ مِنْ سَرِيرِهِ و ذَهَبَ إِلَى الْحَمَّامِ.

"Wow!" he shouted, "I have a brand-new toothbrush! It's blue, my favorite color. Thank you, Mom." He started to brush his teeth.

صَاحَ الْأَخُ الْأَكْبَرُ فَرِحًا : "وَاو!.... صَارَ لَدَيَّ فُرْشَاةُ أَسْنَانٍ جَدِيدَةٍ ! إِنَّها زَرْقَاءُ، و الْأَزْرَقُ لَوْنِيَ الْمُفَضَّلُ. شُكْرًا لَكِ يَا أُمِّي." ثُمَّ بَدَأَ يَفْرُشُ أَسْنَانَهُ.

The middle brother followed him. "I have a new toothbrush as well, and mine's green!" he exclaimed and also began to brush his teeth.

تَبِعَهُ الْأَخُ الْأَوْسَطُ و قَالَ مُتَعَجِّبًا: "أَنَا أَيْضًا أَصْبَحَ لَدَيَّ فُرْشَاةُ أَسْنَانٍ جَدِيدَةٍ ، و لَوْنُهَا أَخْضَرُ." ثُمَّ شَرَعَ هُوَ الْآخَرُ يَفْرُشُ أَسْنَانَهُ.

Jimmy got out of bed and walked slowly towards the bathroom. *Why even bother brushing my teeth?* he thought. *My teeth are fine as they are.*

نَهَضَ جِيمِي مِنْ سَرِيرِهِ و سَارَ بِتَثَاقُل نَحْوَ الْحَمّامِ و هُوَ يَقُولُ فِي نَفْسِهِ: "لَا حَاجَةَ لِأَفْرُشَ أَسْنَانِي، فَهِيَ جَمِيلَةٌ كَمَا هِيَ."

"Look, Jimmy," said his oldest brother, "you have a new toothbrush too. It's orange like your bed."

قَالَ الْأَخُ الْأَكْبَرُ: "أَنْظُرْ يَا جِيمِي، أَنْتَ أَيْضًا لَدَيْكَ فُرْشَاةُ أَسْنَانٍ جَدِيدَةٍ الْآنَ، و لَوْنُهَا بُرْتُقَالِيٌّ كَلَوْنِ سَرِيرِكَ."

"So I have a new toothbrush, big deal." Jimmy stood in front of the mirror, but he still didn't start brushing his teeth.

فَرَدَّ جِيمِي بِلَا مُبَالَاةٍ: "لَدَيَّ فُرْشَاةُ أَسْنَانٍ جَدِيدَةٌ إِذَنْ. يَا لَهُ مِنْ أَمْرٍ مُهِمٍّ." ثُمَّ وَقَفَ أَمَامَ الْمِرْآةِ و لَكِنَّهُ لَمْ يَفْرُشْ أَسْنَانَهُ.

"Kids, hurry up! Breakfast is almost ready," they heard their mother's soft voice. "Has everyone finished brushing their teeth?"

سَمِعَ الْأَرَانِبُ الصِّغَارُ صَوْتَ أُمِّهِمِ الرَّقِيقَ يُنَادِي: "أَسْرِعُوا يَا أَطْفَال، فَالْفَطُورُ يَكَادُ يَجْهَزُ. هَلْ أَنْهَى الْجَمِيعُ تَنْظِيفَ أَسْنَانِهِ؟"

"I've finished," answered the oldest brother and ran out of the bathroom.

أَجَابَ الْأَخُ الْأَكْبَرُ: "لَقَدْ انْتَهَيْتُ مِنْ ذَلِكَ." ثُمَّ خَرَجَ يَجْرِي مِنَ الْحَمَّامِ.

"Me too," replied the middle brother. He ran after his brother to the kitchen.

أَجَابَ الْأَخُ الْأَوْسَطُ : "وَ أَنَا كَذَلِكَ." ثُمَّ رَكَضَ وَرَاءَ أَخِيهِ نَحْوَ الْمَطْبَخِ.

"Mom, I finished brushing my teeth too," shouted Jimmy. He was just about to leave the bathroom, when he heard a voice.

صَاحَ جِيمِي: "أُمِّي، وَ أَنَا أَيْضًا انْتَهَيْتُ مِنْ فَرْشِ أَسْنَانِي." وَ كَانَ عَلَى وَشَكِ مُغَادَرَةِ الْحَمَّامِ، عِنْدَمَا سَمِعَ صَوْتًا.

"It's not nice to lie," the voice said. "You didn't brush your teeth."

قَالَ الصَّوْتُ:"لَيْسَ مِنَ الصَّوَابِ أَنْ تَكْذِبَ. أَنْتَ لَمْ تَفْرُشْ أَسْنَانَكَ."

"Who said that?" asked Jimmy as he looked around in confusion.

سَأَلَ جِيمِي وَ هُوَ يَنْظُرُ حَوْلَهُ فِي ارْتِبَاكٍ:"مَنْ قَالَ ذَلِكَ؟"

Frowning at him was his new orange toothbrush, standing on the counter. He just couldn't believe his eyes...or his ears!

لَمْ يُصَدِّقْ جِيمِي عَيْنَيْهِ و أُذُنَيْهِ عِنْدَمَا رَأَى أَمَامَهُ فَرْشَاةَ أَسْنَانِهِ الْبُرْتُقَالِيَّةَ الْجَدِيدَةَ وَاقِفَةً عِنْدَ الْحَوْضِ تَنْظُرُ إِلَيْهِ فِي عُبُوسٍ.

"A toothbrush can't talk," he said in a stunned voice.

قَالَ جِيمِي بِصَوْتٍ مَشْدُوهٍ:"فُرْشَاةُ الْأَسْنَانِ لَا تَسْتَطِيعُ الْكَلَامَ."

"I sure can. I'm a magical toothbrush," said the toothbrush proudly. "My job is to make sure EVERYONE brushes his teeth."

قَالَتْ فُرْشَاةُ الْأَسْنَانِ بِفَخْرٍ:" بِالتَّأْكِيدِ أَسْتَطِيعُ. أَنَا فُرْشَاةُ أَسْنَانٍ سِحْرِيَّةٍ، و وَاجِبِي هُوَ أَنْ أَتَأَكَّدَ أَنَّ الْكُلَّ يَفْرُشُ أَسْنَانَهُ."

Jimmy laughed in response. "I didn't brush my teeth and nothing bad happened to me."

أَجَابَ "جِيمِي" ضَاحِكًا:" أَنَا لَمْ أَفْرُشْ أَسْنَانِي و لَمْ يُصِبْنِي سُوءٌ."

"Look at yourself," the brush said. "Your teeth are yellow and your breath smells terrible."

قَالَتِ الْفُرْشَاةُ:" أُنْظُرْ إِلَى نَفْسِكَ. أَسْنَانُكَ مُصْفَرَّةٌ و رَائِحَةُ أَنْفَاسِكَ كَرِيهَةٌ."

"That's not true, brush. You're just making it up!" Jimmy took the toothbrush and threw it far into the corner of the bathroom.

فَقَالَ جِيمِي: "هَذَا لَيْسَ صَحِيحًا. أَنْتِ تَخْتَلِقِينَ ذَلِكَ!" ثُمَّ أَخَذَ الْفُرْشَاةَ و أَلْقَى بِهَا بَعِيدًا فِي رُكْنِ الْحَمَّامِ.

Then he ran into the kitchen to have his breakfast.

و بَعْدَ ذَلِكَ رَكَضَ إِلَى الْمَطْبَخِ لِيَتَنَاوَلَ فَطُورَهُ.

"That's no way to treat me," shouted the toothbrush. "I'm a magical toothbrush. I'll prove how important I am!"

صَرَخَتِ الْفُرْشَاةُ: "لَمْ يَكُنْ عَلَيْكَ أَنْ تُعَامِلَني هَكَذَا. أَنَا فُرْشَاةُ أَسْنَانٍ سِحْرِيَّةٌ، و سَوْفَ أُثْبِتُ مَدَى أَهَمِّيَّتي!"

By this time, Jimmy was already sitting down next to his brothers in the kitchen.

فِي هَذِهِ الْأَثْنَاءِ، انْضَمَّ جِيمِي إِلَى شَقِيقَيْهِ فِي الْمَطْبَخِ.

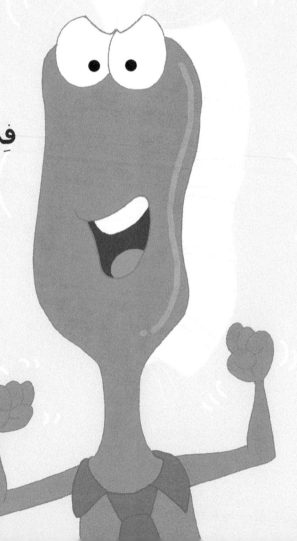

He took a sandwich and brought it to his mouth.
But then the sandwich jumped out of Jimmy's
hands right onto the plate of his oldest brother.

أَخَذَ جِيمِي شَطِيرَةً و قَرَّبَهَا إِلَى فَمِهِ، و لَكِنَّ الشَّطِيرَةَ انْفَلَتَتْ مِنْ يَدَيْهِ و قَفَزَتْ إِلَى طَبَقِ شَقِيقِهِ الْأَكْبَرِ.

Instead of the sandwich, Jimmy had bitten his fingers — hard!

و بَدَلًا عَنِ الشّطِيرَةِ، عَضَّ جِيمِي أَصَابِعَهُ بِقُوَّةٍ.

"Who does this sandwich belong to?" the brother asked.

سَأَلَ الْأَخُ الْأَكْبَرُ:"شَطِيرَةُ مَنْ هَذِهِ؟"

"My sandwich ran away from me," answered Jimmy. "It's mine!"

أَجَابَ جِيمِي: "لَقَدْ فَرَّتْ شَطِيرَتِي مِنِّي. إِنَّهَا لِي!"

"Quite an imagination you have, sweetie. How can a sandwich run away?" his mother said.

فَقَالَتْ أُمُّهُ: "مُخَيِّلَتُكَ وَاسِعَةٌ يَا عَزِيزِي. كَيْفَ يُمْكِنُ لِشَطِيرَةٍ أَنْ تَفِرَّ هَارِبَةً؟"

"I don't know how, but that's really what happened," said Jimmy.

قَالَ جِيمِي:" أَنَا لَا أَعْرِفُ كَيْفَ، و لَكِنَّ هَذَا مَا حَصَلَ فِعْلًا."

Then, Mom gave him a big plate full of salad. "Here, perhaps you would like to eat a delicious vegetable salad instead," she said.

بَعْدَ ذَلِكَ، قَدَّمَتْ لَهُ الْأُمّ طَبَقًا كَبِيرًا مَلِيئًا بِالسَّلَطَةِ وَ قَالَتْ: "تَفَضَّلْ، رُبَّمَا تُرِيدُ تَنَاوُلَ سَلَطَةِ خُضَارٍ عِوَضًا عَنِ الشَّطِيرَةِ."

"Yummy, I love vegetable salad," said Jimmy, about to start eating. Suddenly, the salad plate leaped up and settled down on the table near his middle brother.

قَالَ جِيمِي : "تَبْدُو لَذِيذَةً...أَنَا أُحِبُّ سَلَطَةَ الْخُضَارِ". وقَبْلَ أَنْ يَبْدَأَ بِالْأَكْلِ قَفَزَ طَبَقُ السَّلَطَةِ فَجْأَةً و اسْتَقَرَّ عَلَى الطَّاوِلَةِ عِنْدَ شَقِيقِ جِيمِي الْأَوْسَطِ.

"Look," said the middle brother, "how did your plate get over here?"

قَالَ الْأَخُ الْأَوْسَطُ: "اُنْظُرْ! كَيْفَ جَاءَ طَبَقُكَ إِلَى هُنَا؟"

"You were right, honey! Your food is running away from you!" said their astonished mom. "That's strange."

قَالَتِ الْأُمُّ بِانْدِهَاشٍ: "لَقَدْ كُنْتَ مُحِقًّا يَا عَزِيزِي! إِنَّ طَعَامَكَ يَهْرُبُ مِنْكَ. هَذَا غَرِيبٌ!"

"Mom, I'm getting hungry already. What can I eat?" said Jimmy.

قَالَ جِيمِي: "أُمِّي، أَنَا جَائِعٌ. مَاذَا يُمْكِنُنِي أَنْ آكُلَ؟"

Mom thought for a moment. "How about your favorite carrot cake? I'll give you a big slice."

فَكَّرَتِ الْأُمُّ لِلَحْظَةٍ و قَالَتْ: "مَاذَا عَنْ كَعْكَةِ الْجَزَرِ الَّتِي تُحِبُّهَا؟ سَأُعْطِيكَ شَرِيحَةً كَبِيرَةً."

"Oh yes, carrot cake! I love it so much," Jimmy shouted happily, "Thanks, Mom."

صَاحَ جِيمِي والسَّعَادَةُ تَغْمُرُهُ: "أَجَلْ، أَجَلْ، كَعْكَةُ الْجَزَرِ! أَنَا أُحِبُّهَا كَثِيرًا! شُكْرًا لَكِ يَا أَمِّي!"

However, before Jimmy could take the cake, it began float in the air. It flew into the living room and settled on the couch.

ولَكِنْ قَبْلَ أَنْ يَتَمَكَّنَ جِيمِي مِنْ أَخْذِ الْكَعْكَةِ، بَدَأَتْ تَطْفُو فِي الْهَوَاءِ و طَارَتْ إِلَى غُرْفَةِ الْجُلُوسِ ثُمَّ اسْتَقَرَّتْ عَلَى الْأَرِيكَةِ.

Jimmy hopped out of his chair and started chasing the piece of cake.

قَفَزَ جِيمِي مِنْ مَقْعَدِهِ و بَدَأَ بِمُلَاحَقَةِ قِطْعَةِ الكَعْكِ.

He jumped on the sofa, but the cake zoomed back to the table. Jimmy ran back to the table and then the cake flew out of the house. Jimmy rushed after it.

نَطَّ عَلَى الْأَرِيكَةِ ، و لَكِنَّ الْكَعْكَةَ قَفَزَتْ ثَانِيَةً نَحْوَ الطَّاوِلَةِ . لَحِقَ جِيمِي بِهَا فَطَارَتِ الْكَعْكَةُ إِلَى خَارِجِ الْبَيْتِ، وهَرَعَ الْأَرْنَبُ الصَّغِيرُ مُسْرِعًا خَلْفَهَا.

The cake looped around the house while Jimmy trailed behind it. Another round and another and another, and still Jimmy followed.

حَلَّقَتِ الْكَعْكَةُ هُنَا و هُنَاكَ لِوَقْتٍ طَوِيلٍ حَوْلَ الْبَيْتِ بَيْنَمَا اسْتَمَرَّ جِيمِي فِي مُلَاحَقَتِهَا أَيْنَمَا ذَهَبَتْ.

Until he had run out of breath. Tired, Jimmy sat down at the entrance of the house and started crying.

بَعْدَ أَنْ نَالَ مِنْهُ التَّعَبُ ، جَلَسَ جِيمِي عِنْدَ مَدْخَلِ الْبَيْتِ و بَدَأ يَبْكِي.

At the same moment, two of his friends were passing by. "Hey, Jimmy," they greeted. "Why are you sitting here looking so sad? Come play with us."

فِي تِلْكَ اللَّحْظَةِ ، مَرَّ عَلَيْهِ صَدِيقَانِ لَهُ و أَلْقَيَا عَلَيْهِ التَّحِيَّةَ قَائِلَيْنِ:" مَرْحَبًا جِيمِي ، لِمَاذَا تَجْلِسُ وَحِيدًا هُنَا و عَلَى وَجْهِكَ عَلَامَاتُ الْحُزْنِ؟ تَعَالَ و الْعَبْ مَعَنَا."

"Yes, I'd like that!" Jimmy ran towards them.
"You won't believe what happened to me today!"

رَكَضَ جِيمِي نَحْوَهُمَا قَائِلًا: "أَجَلْ ، أَنَا أَرْغَبُ فِي ذَلِكَ. لَنْ تُصَدِّقَا
مَا حَصَلَ مَعِي الْيَوْمَ!"

But, as he opened his mouth, the friends shouted,

وَ لَكِنْ ، فِي اللَّحْظَةِ الَّتِي فَتَحَ فِيهَا
جِيمِي فَمَهُ، صَاحَ الصَّدِيقَانِ.

"Yikes, what a stink! We'll go play somewhere else while you go brush your teeth!" With that, they ran away.

قَالَا :" يَا لِلْقَرَفِ! مَا هَذِهِ الرَّائِحَةُ الْفَظِيعَةُ؟ سَنَلْعَبُ فِي مَكَانٍ آخَرَ بَيْنَمَا تَفْرِشُ أَنْتَ أَسْنَانَكَ."

Bursting into tears yet again, Jimmy entered the house.

دَخَل جِيمِي الْمَنْزِلَ و قَدْ انْفَجَرَ باكِيًا مُجَدَّدًا.

He went to the bathroom and saw the magical toothbrush flying in the air, smiling kindly at him. "Hello, Jimmy. I've been waiting for you. Do you want to brush your teeth now?"

دَخَلَ الْحَمَّامَ و رَأَى فُرْشَاةَ الْأَسْنَانِ السِّحْرِيَّةَ تُحَلِّقُ فِي الْهَوَاءِ و هِيَ تَبْتَسِمُ لَهُ بِلُطْف. قَالَت الْفُرْشَاةُ : "مَرْحَبًا يَا جِيمِي، كُنْتُ بِانْتِظَارِكَ. هَلْ تُرِيدُ أَنْ تُنَظِّفَ أَسْنَانَكَ الْآنَ؟"

Jimmy started brushing his teeth, from one side to the other, top and bottom, front and back. He brushed them until they became white and shiny.

بَدَأَ جِيمِي يَفْرُشُ أَسْنَانَهُ بِعِنَايَةٍ. فَرَشَ الْجَانِبَ الْأَيْمَنَ و الْأَيْسَرَ، الْفَكَّ الْأَعْلَى و الْأَسْفَلَ، الْأَسْنَانَ الْأَمَامِيَّةَ ثُمَّ الْخَلْفِيَّةَ، حتَّى أَصْبَحَتْ أَسْنَانُهُ بَيْضَاءَ و لَامِعَةً.

Gazing proudly at his reflection in the mirror, Jimmy said, "Thank you, brush. It was even nice and pleasant to brush my teeth."

قالَ جيمي و هُوَ يَنظُرُ بِفَخرٍ إلَى انعِكاسِ صُورَتِه في الْمِرآةِ: "شُكراً لكِ أيتُها الْفُرْشاةِ. لَقَدْ كانَ تَنْظيفُ أَسْنانِي جَميلاً و مُمتِعًا."

"You look great," said the brush. "By the way, my name is Leah. I'm always here to help."

قالَت الْفُرْشاةُ :"أَنْتَ تَبْدُو رائِعًا. بِالمُناسَبَةِ، اسْمِي "لِيَا" وَ أَنَا مُسْتَعِدَةٌ لِمُساعَدَتِكَ دائِمًا."

That's how Jimmy and Leah became good friends. Ever since that day, they've seen each other twice a day to protect Jimmy's teeth and help them grow strong and healthy.

و هَكَذا أَصْبَحَ جيمي و لِيا صَديقَيْنِ. و مُنذُ ذَلِكَ الْيَوْمِ صَارا يَلْتَقِيانِ مَرَّتَيْنِ يَوْمِيًا لِيَحْمِيا أَسْنانَ جيمِي وَ يُساعِدانِها عَلَى النمُوّ لِتُصْبِحَ قويَّةً و صِحيَّةً.

CPSIA information can be obtained
at www.ICGtesting.com
Printed in the USA
LVHW07*1708060918
589366LV00029B/544/P

9 781525 904714